31192020404040

USING THERMOMETERS

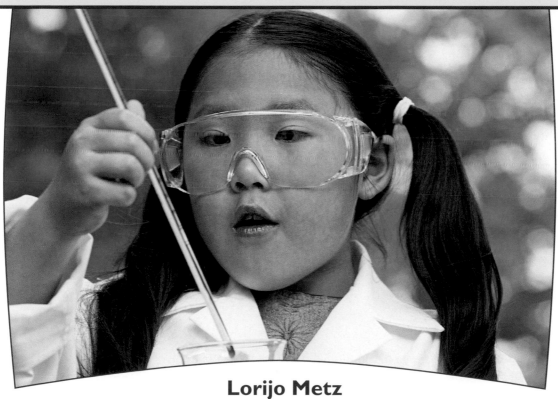

Lorijo Metz

PowerKiDS press

New York

Dedicated to Kathleen Stevens, may your coffee always be the perfect temperature

Published in 2013 by The Rosen Publishing Group, Inc.
29 East 21st Street, New York, NY 10010

First Edition

Editor: Amelie von Zumbusch
Book Design: Kate Laczynski

Photo Credits: Cover, p. 5 Image Source/Getty Images; pp. 4, 7 (right), 11 (bottom), 14 iStockphoto/Thinkstock; p. 6 Science & Society Picture Library/SSPL/Getty Images; p. 7 (left) Ottavio Mario Leoni/The Bridgeman Art Library/Getty Images; p. 8 Monty Rakusen/Cultura/Getty Images; p. 9 Konstantin Shevtsov/Shutterstock.com; p. 10 © iStockphoto.com/malerapaso; pp. 11 (top), 13 Curve/the Agency Collection/Getty Images; p. 15 poonsap/Shutterstock.com; p. 16 Tim Ridley/Dorling Kindersley/Getty Images; p. 17 Moirenc Camille/hemis.fr/Getty Images; p. 18 Simone van den Berg/Shutterstock.com; p. 19 (left) © iStockphoto.com/Patrick Poendl; p. 19 (right) Monik/Shutterstock.com; p. 21 Image Source/Thinkstock; p. 22 (top) Leslie Miller/age fotostock/Getty Images; p. 22 (bottom) Palmer Kane LLC/Shutterstock.com.

Library of Congress Cataloging-in-Publication Data

Metz, Lorijo.
  Using thermometers / by Lorijo Metz. — 1st ed.
      p. cm. — (Science tools)
  Includes index.
  ISBN 978-1-4488-9684-4 (library binding) — ISBN 978-1-4488-9826-8 (pbk.) —
  ISBN 978-1-4488-9827-5 (6-pack)
  1. Thermometers—Juvenile literature. I. Title.
  QC271.4.M48 2013
  536'.50287—dc23

                                    2012027661

Manufactured in the United States of America

CPSIA Compliance Information: Batch #W13PK4: For Further Information contact Rosen Publishing, New York, New York at 1-800-237-9932

CONTENTS

Have you ever run outside on a sunny day expecting it to be warm but found that it was cold? Things like snow and light give us a clue to **temperature**, or how hot or cold something is. However, you cannot see temperature. Luckily, you can measure it. The most common way is with a thermometer.

A meat thermometer lets cooks know if meat is done cooking.

Many science experiments require a thermometer.

People need to measure temperature for many reasons. They use different kinds of thermometers to measure it. Bakers use oven thermometers to measure how hot their ovens are. Scientists, doctors, and cooks all depend on thermometers. Have you ever used a thermometer in a science **experiment**?

A Matter of Temperature

THERMOSCOPE

Air in upper bulb

Glass neck

Colored water in lower bulb

Everything, including you, is made of **matter**. Matter is made of very small parts called **atoms**. Though atoms are too small to see, you can tell if they are moving fast or slow. Atoms moving quickly have more energy and produce more heat.

In 1592, the Italian scientist Galileo invented the first thermometer. His thermometer, called a **thermoscope**, contained colored water and air. When atoms of air slow down, they produce less heat. With less movement, they take up less space.

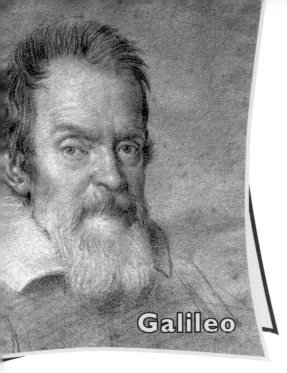

Galileo

Bulb

Weighted temperature tag

Galileo used this to show change in temperature. As air in the top of his thermoscope cooled, colored water moved up the neck to fill in the space.

Bulb that tells the temperature

Galileo's students invented the Galilean thermometer. The bottoms of the floating bulbs tell you what the temperature is.

7

Fahrenheit and Celsius

In 1724, Daniel Gabriel Fahrenheit invented the first standard **scale**, or way of measuring temperature. He placed a thermometer filled with **alcohol** in a bowl filled with the coldest mix of ice, salt, and water he could make. He labeled the point that the alcohol rose to 0 **degrees**. The ° symbol often stands for "degrees."

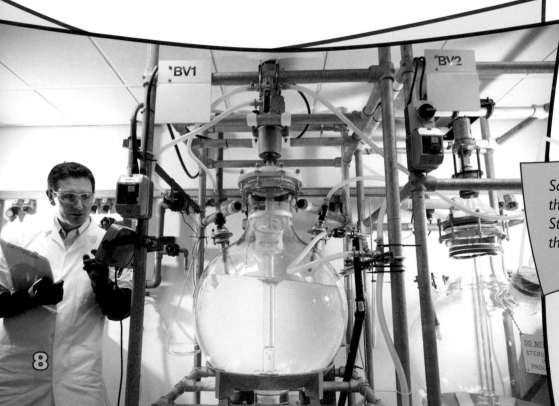

Scientists, including those in the United States, tend to use the Celsius scale.

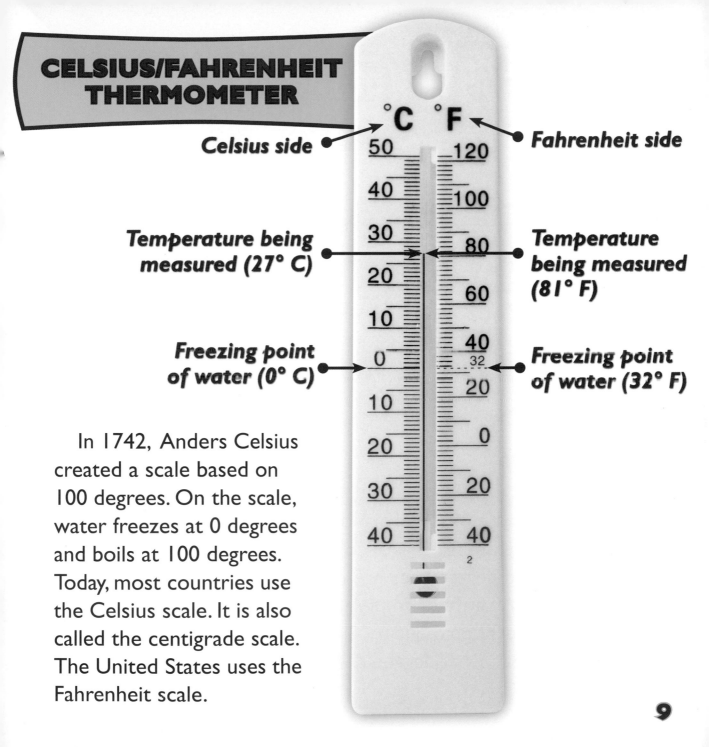

°C   °F

Celsius side

Fahrenheit side

Temperature being measured (27° C)

Temperature being measured (81° F)

Freezing point of water (0° C)

Freezing point of water (32° F)

In 1742, Anders Celsius created a scale based on 100 degrees. On the scale, water freezes at 0 degrees and boils at 100 degrees. Today, most countries use the Celsius scale. It is also called the centigrade scale. The United States uses the Fahrenheit scale.

More than One Kind of Thermometer

DIGITAL THERMOMETER
button
98.0°F
Measuring tip
Display screen

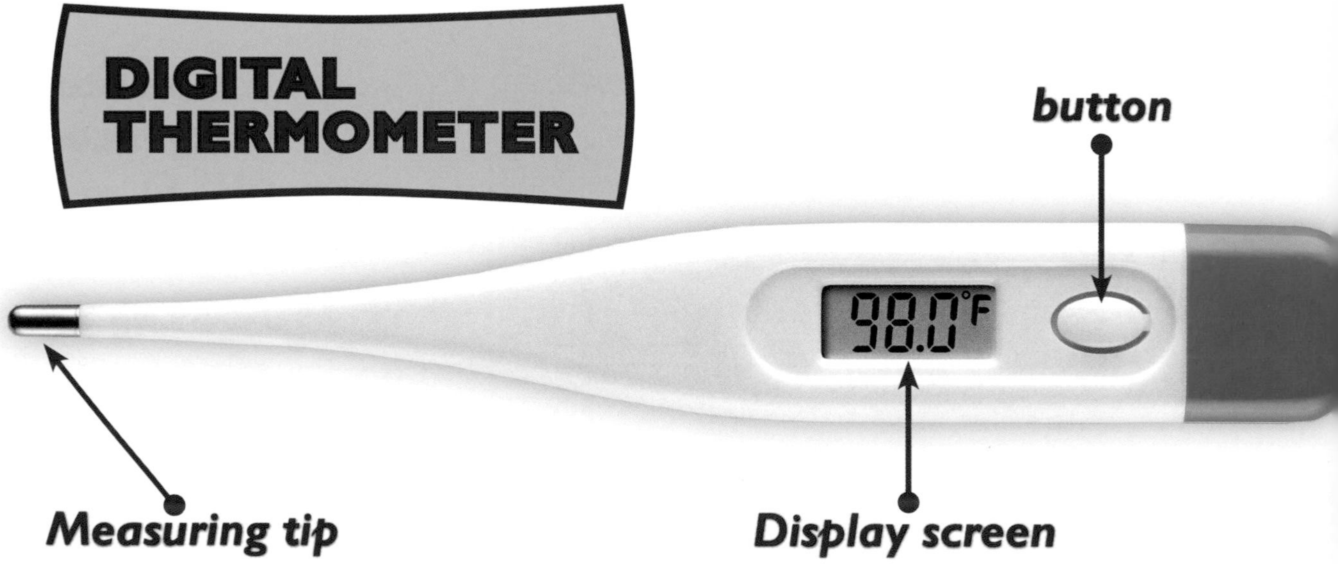

Most thermometers are thin glass tubes with bulbs on the bottom filled with colored alcohol or **mercury**. Numbered degree lines are marked along the side or on the glass. When the temperature increases, the liquid inside has nowhere to go but up. Since the liquid is colored, it is easy to read what degree it stops by.

Digital thermometers measure temperature with an electric sensor called a **thermocouple**. The temperature is displayed on a screen.

Spring thermometers look like clocks that show temperature instead of time. They use a metal spring that changes size with the temperature. An arm attached to the spring points to the temperature.

This student is using a glass thermometer in her science experiment.

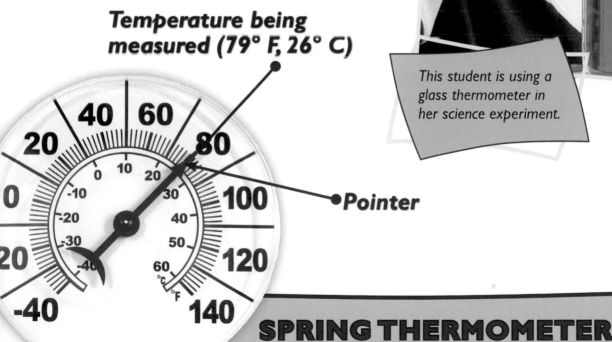

Temperature being measured (79° F, 26° C)

●**Pointer**

SPRING THERMOMETER

Safety and Thermometers

Mercury is a silver-colored metal that is liquid at room temperature. Enclosed in glass, mercury is safe. However, mercury is harmful when breathed or touched. If you break a mercury thermometer, do not touch the mercury or the broken glass. Call an adult. Make sure everyone stays away from the area. Adults can check with the Environmental Protection Agency, or EPA, to learn more about cleaning up a mercury spill.

Always follow science safety rules when doing an experiment. If you are measuring the temperature of chemicals, remember to wear goggles.

Use care when handling other glass thermometers as well. Broken glass is sharp and can easily cut you. Always ask an adult to help you clean up a broken glass thermometer.

Scientists do experiments to study how temperature affects things. Do you think that apples stored in refrigerators or apples stored at room temperature stay fresh longer? To test this question, you might use four apples of the same size and type. The only thing that should be different about the apples is the temperatures at which they will be stored.

There are several types of apples. Make sure to use apples of the same type in your experiment.

Scientists call the facts they record in their logs data.

Place two apples on the counter and two in the refrigerator. Measure the temperature at each place with a thermometer.

Note the temperatures in a **log**. Check the apples at the same time of day for several days. Describe them in your log. What difference does temperature make?

15

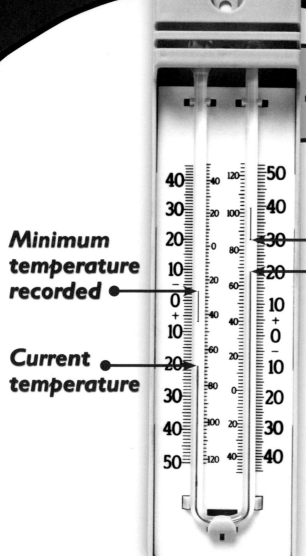

MAXIMUM-MINIMUM THERMOMETER

Minimum temperature recorded

Current temperature

Maximum temperature recorded

Current temperature

Scientists use a maximum-minimum thermometer to study the weather. This type of thermometer uses two glass thermometers placed side by side. One thermometer measures the highest temperature. The other thermometer measures the lowest temperature.

Scientists keep a log of these temperatures. Over time, the log helps them **forecast**, or make an educated guess about what the temperature of an area will be like in any given month. For example, they know that some places, like the North Pole, are usually cold most of the year. Other places, like Chicago, Illinois, tend to be warmest in the month of July.

Scientists at weather stations, such as this one in Vaucluse, France, record many kinds of weather information. This includes maximum and minimum daily temperatures.

Temperature and States of Matter

The three main **states**, or forms, of matter are solid, liquid, and gas. What state matter is in can tell us a lot about its temperature. Liquids have set boiling points, or temperatures at which they become gases. The point at which a liquid becomes a solid is its freezing point.

The temperature at which water boils also depends on how far above sea level you are. Water boils at a lower temperature high in the mountains.

GLASS THERMOMETER

This melting iceberg will become part of the ocean. The clouds above it formed when water vapor cooled and formed water droplets.

°C °F

$^1/_1$ $^2/_1$

Freezing point of phosphorous ● 50 → 40 120 — 100

Freezing point of cesium ● 30 → 80 — 20 60

Freezing point of seawater ● 0 → 10 — 40 20 0 20 30 — 20

Celsius based his temperature scale on the freezing and boiling points of water. We know if the temperature drops to 0° Celsius (32° F), water becomes ice. As the temperature rises, water turns back into a liquid. When water reaches 100° Celsius (212° F), it boils and turns into a gas called water vapor.

Body Temperature

People and many other animals are **warm-blooded**. The energy we get from the food we eat keeps our bodies at a constant temperature. Healthy people have a temperature of around 98.6° F (37° C). Knowing this, doctors can use a thermometer to measure whether our temperature is too high or too low. Higher temperatures mean we are sick. If our temperature is too low, our bodies can stop working.

We use thermometers to do everything from forecasting the weather to keeping our ovens at the perfect temperature for baking a cake. They are helpful in so many ways!

If a kid's temperature is more than 99.5° F (37.5° C) when it is measured with a thermometer that goes in the mouth, that kid has a fever.

Now it is your turn to study temperature like a scientist. Below is what you need:

1. A notebook or lined piece of paper to keep a log on
2. Something to write with
3. An outdoor thermometer

For the next two days, record the outdoor temperature in your log in the morning, afternoon, and evening. Record the temperature at the same time each day. Beside each temperature, take notes about what you notice. What patterns do you see? For example, what things look or even sound different when the temperature is cooler? What things stay the same?

GLOSSARY

alcohol (AL-kuh-hol) A clear fuel that pours and burns easily.

atoms (A-temz) The smallest parts of elements.

degrees (dih-GREEZ) Measurements of how hot or cold something is.

experiment (ik-SPER-uh-ment) A set of actions or steps taken to learn more about something.

forecast (FOR-kast) To figure out when something will happen.

log (LOG) A record of day-to-day activities.

matter (MA-ter) Anything that has weight and takes up space.

mercury (MER-kyuh-ree) A poisonous, silver-colored element.

scale (SKAYL) A standard system for measuring something.

states (STAYTS) Forms that matter can take, such as solid, liquid, or gas.

temperature (TEM-pur-cher) How hot or cold something is.

thermocouple (ther-muh-KUH-pel) An electrical sensor that measures heat.

thermoscope (THER-muh-skohp) An early kind of thermometer.

warm-blooded (WORM-bluh-did) Having a body heat that stays the same, no matter how warm or cold the surroundings are.

INDEX

WEBSITES

Due to the changing nature of Internet links, PowerKids Press has developed an online list of websites related to the subject of this book. This site is updated regularly. Please use this link to access the list:
www.powerkidslinks.com/scto/therm/